Shapes around Town

Stars
around Town

by Nathan Olson

Capstone
press

Mankato, Minnesota

A+ Books are published by Capstone Press,
151 Good Counsel Drive, P.O. Box 669, Mankato, Minnesota 56002.
www.capstonepress.com

1 2 3 4 5 6 11 10 09 08 07 06

Library of Congress Cataloging-in-Publication Data
Olson, Nathan.
    Stars around town / by Nathan Olson.
    p. cm.—(A+ books. Shapes around town)
    Summary: "Simple text, photographs, and illustrations help readers identify stars that can be found
in a city"—Provided by publisher.
    Includes bibliographical references and index.
    ISBN-13: 978-0-7368-6372-8 (hardcover)
    ISBN-10: 0-7368-6372-9 (hardcover)
    1. Stars (Shape)—Juvenile literature. 2. Shapes—Juvenile literature. I. Title. II. Series.
    QA482.O475 2007
    516'.154—dc22   2005036514

Credits

Jenny Marks, editor; Kia Adams, designer; Renée Doyle, illustrator; Kelly Garvin,
    photo researcher/photo editor

Photo Credits

Corbis/Ariel Skelley, 18–19; Gabe Palmer, 22; Henry Diltz, 10, 16; Jan Butchofsky-Houser, 9;
    Jon Hicks, 12; Mark E. Gibson, 4–5; Nick Gunderson, 8; Owen Franken, 17; Paul A. Souders, 14;
    Richard Cummins, 13, 23; Rick Gayle Studio, 15; zefa/K. Hackenberg, 24–25
Getty Images Inc./The Image Bank/Jeremy Walker, 11
NAVA, 26–27 (all)
Shutterstock/Erik H. Pronske, M.D., 6
SuperStock/age fotostock, 21; David Muscroft, 7; Kwame Zikomo, 20; Richard Cummins, cover

Note to Parents, Teachers, and Librarians

The Shapes around Town set uses color photographs and a nonfiction format to introduce readers to
the shapes around them. *Stars around Town* is designed to be read aloud to a pre-reader, or to be
read independently by an early reader. Images and activities help early readers and listeners perceive
and recognize shapes. The book encourages further learning by including the following sections: Table
of Contents, Flags with Stars, Welcome to Star Town, Glossary, Read More, Internet Sites, and Index.
Early readers may need assistance using these features.

Table of Contents

What Is a Star?

Stars are shapes with at least five points. Let's look around to find stars all over town.

TEXAS STATE H

4

This five pointed star hangs high above a city street. Most stars have five points.

Some stars have six or more points. The highway patrol's star has seven golden points.

Stars High and Low

This star twinkles in the city at night. A string of tiny lights makes this giant star glow.

8

Look down at the city sidewalk.
You might just spy stars right
under your own two feet.

Stars can appear almost anywhere in a city. What do these stars decorate?

10

In the winter, you may see
a special tree topped with a star.
What kind of tree could it be?

This star is made out of a
strong metal called iron. How
many points does this star have?

Stars appear in places where
you can watch movies or
other shows.

Stars shine bright in this neon sign. Neon is a special gas that lights up.

Signs high in the air invite people to stop and shop. How many stars do you count on this sign?

COURAGE

THE STAR

A star on a sign gives the message that this is a special place to visit.

Stars are symbols for things that are big or special. This mall has more than 500 stores!

Fun Stars

Stars show up all over town in summertime. Summer parades march up and down city streets.

Stars made of chalk decorate neighborhood streets. But they disappear when it rains.

Some people wear stars. Who is wearing stars and who is not?

Hot dogs are the stars of the menu at the lunch cart in the city park.

HOT DOGS
plain   1.50
w/ onions   1.75
w/ kraut   1.75
w/ cheese   2.00
w/ chili   2.00
soda   .75
chips   .50
candy   .75

Stars light the night at outdoor
restaurants along city sidewalks.

Lights glitter up and down city streets. They shine with points of light that look like twinkling stars.

Flags with Stars

Stars decorate many flags that proudly say "this city is special." How many stars do each of these flags have?

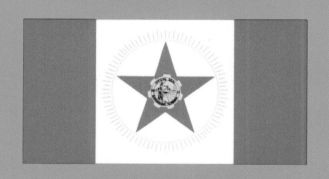

Birmingham, Alabama

Washington, D.C.

Springfield, Illinois

Richmond, Virginia

Chicago, Illinois

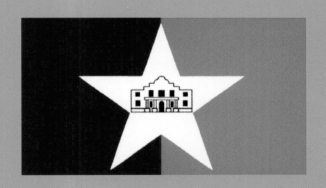

San Antonio, Texas

Detroit, Michigan

Jackson, Mississippi

Louisville, Kentucky

Welcome to Star Town

Circus
of the
Stars

Star Town is full of star shapes both big and small. Where do you see stars?

Glossary

decorate (DEK-uh-rate)—to add things to make something prettier or stand out more

highway patrol (HYE-way puh-TROHL)—a police officer who protects and watches over people who are driving on highways

iron (EYE-urn)—a strong, hard metal

neon (NEE-on)—a colorless, odorless gas; neon is used to make some lights and signs glow.

shape (SHAYP)—a form or outline

symbol (SIM-buhl)—a design that stands for something else

twinkle (TWING-kuhl)—to shine with quick flashes of light

Read More

Burke, Jennifer S. *Stars.* City Shapes. New York: Children's Press, 2000.

Salzmann, Mary Elizabeth. *Stars.* What Shape Is It? Edina, Minn.: Abdo, 2000.

Schuette, Sarah L. *Stars.* Shapes. Mankato, Minn.: Capstone Press, 2003.

Internet Sites

FactHound offers a safe, fun way to find Internet sites related to this book. All of the sites on FactHound have been researched by our staff.

Here's how:

1. Go to *www.facthound.com*
2. Select your grade level.
3. Type in this book ID **0736863729** for age-appropriate sites. You may also browse subjects by clicking on the letters, or by clicking on pictures and words.
4. Click on the **Fetch It** button.

FactHound will fetch the best sites for you!

Index